THE STORY OF DIAMONDS

THE STORY OF DIAMONDS

JEAN MILNE

LINNET BOOKS
2000

First published 2000 as a Linnet Book,
an imprint of The Shoe String Press, Inc.,
2 Linsley Street, North Haven, Connecticut 06473.

Milne, Jean, 1920–
    The story of diamonds / by Jean Milne.
       p. cm.
    Includes bibliographical references and index.
    Summary: Discusses the history, scientific makeup, and
cultural significance of diamonds, their uses, and stories about
famous diamonds.
    ISBN 0-208-02476-X (library bdg. : alk. paper)
    1. Diamonds Juvenile literature.   [1. Diamonds.]   I. Title.
QE393.M55   1999
553.8'2—dc21   99-36426
                                                            CIP

The paper in this publication meets the minimum requirements
of American National Standard for Information Sciences—
Permanence of Paper for Printed Library Materials,
ANSI Z39.48-1984.

Designed by Sanna Stanley

Printed in the United States of America

CONTENTS

1.

WHAT IS A DIAMOND?

To most people, a diamond is a flashy stone set in a ring or other jewelry. They would be shocked if you told them it was nothing more than a piece of carbon—yes, the same thing as the soft graphite in our ordinary pencil, or the ashes left after a fire.

Though the most precious of gems, the diamond is composed of one of the most common substances on earth. Carbon is found in all living things, plants as well as animals, and in many rocks. Diamonds were formed deep inside the earth by tremendous heat and pressure. Thus, the carbon atoms were squeezed tightly together, making the crystal structure of the diamond very different from that of graphite. The diamond is the hardest natural substance ever discovered, nearly 150 times harder than the world's second hardest mineral, corundum. People soon learned that it was so hard that only another diamond could be used to polish the stone.

Because of its hardness, the ancients considered it indestructible. The word "diamond" actually comes from a Greek word, *adamas*, meaning "invincible" or "unconquerable." Hardness, though, only means resistance to scratching or chipping.

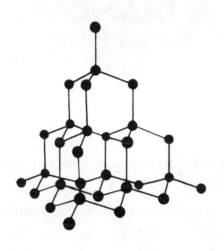

The atomic structure of diamonds is a system of interfacing hexagons with each carbon atom linked to four others.

We know today that, because there is some variation in the arrangement of the carbon atoms in diamonds, there is also some variation in the hardness of the diamonds found in different mines. Also, some stones resist scratching by another diamond in some directions more than others. Many good gemstones were ruined before it became known that a diamond, though hard, is very brittle and can be broken by a blow from a hammer or other heavy object, or by just dropping it on a hard surface.

Not even the strongest acids will affect a diamond, but it will burn in intense heat, disappearing as the colorless gas, carbon dioxide. Besides being the only gemstone composed of a single element, it is also the only combustible one.

It is strange that this stone was so highly regarded in ancient times, before anyone knew how to cut gemstones. In its natural state it doesn't look special at all. Stones found above

Diamonds in the rough. Courtesy of the Diamond Information Center on behalf of De Beers.

ground are usually grayish and sometimes look like just a dull or slightly waxy or greasy pebble. Crude polishing reveals little of their brilliance.

The diamond is the most perfectly crystallized of minerals, with more or less regular faces. The most common shape is an octahedron, which has eight faces. It looks like two square-based pyramids with their bases put together. The next most common shape is a dodecahedron, which has twelve faces. Cubes and even rough spheres have been found, and one crystal, called a dog's tooth, is long, slightly curved, and has one blunt end and one pointed one. Different shapes come about because of the arrangement of atoms within each individual crystal. Sometimes two or three crystals are found joined together.

The crystals can be transparent, translucent (allowing some light to pass through them), or opaque (permitting no passage of light). The opaque are the most commonly found.

ſPECIAL OPTICAL PROPERTIEſ

How can a completely colorless gem be so absolutely beautiful? It is the skill of the gem cutter, of course, that reveals its great beauty, but the basic optical properties are in the rough stone itself.

Diamonds are special because of their brilliance, or luster, and their "fire" (flashes of separate colors). The brilliance is due to the stone's high refractive index, far higher than that of other popular gems, such as the emerald. The diamond's refractive quality (light-bending ability) enables a well-cut stone to throw back almost all the light that enters it. A few minerals such as titanite and zircon have a higher index of refraction, but although they have been used as gems, they are not as valuable, because they can be chipped and scratched easily. The "fire" is due to the stone's "dispersion," its ability to split white light into its spectrum colors.

As you have probably noticed, when you look at a diamond, its brilliance and its fire are increased by movement of the stone.

When diamonds are exposed to ultraviolet light, they fall into three distinct types: those which do not glow or fluoresce; those that are fluorescent but cease to glow when the light is removed; and those that are phosphorescent and continue to glow for a long time. Unlike the first two, the latter, which contain a small amount of boron, are good conductors of electricity.

The most common colors given off under ultraviolet light are blue or mauve, but colors will vary from stone to stone. Some pink diamonds have a bright orange glow, and the famous blue Hope diamond gives off red.

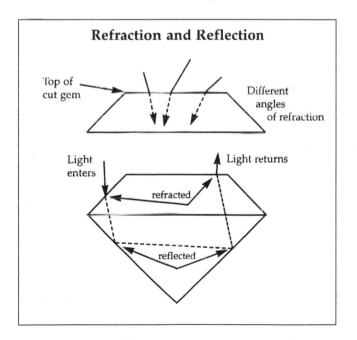

The refraction, or bending, of light entering and exiting a cut diamond gives the stone its brillance.

GEM OF MANY COLORS

The diamond is the only colorless gemstone that has great beauty, and generally the less color the better. Although they are actually colorless, the best stones are called "blue-white."

An impurity in the diamond crystal will give it a tinge of color. Even a small amount of nitrogen will add a yellowish tone, and a larger amount produces green or greenish-black. A small amount of boron creates a pale blue.

Slightly-tinted stones are called "off-color" and are of much less value than a "blue-white." When there is a high concentration of color, however, a diamond is called a "fancy." Because such colored diamonds are extremely rare, they can be much more valuable than the perfectly colorless stone.

Diamonds are found in a wide range of colors. The rarest and usually most valuable are the sapphire-blue, deep red, pink, canary-yellow, and violet. The most common colored stones are black and various greens. In between are such popular shades as emerald green, apple green, violet-blue, light blue, golden brown, and cinnamon. Although most orange diamonds are not considered attractive, an exceptionally fine one sold at an auction in 1997 for 1.3 million dollars.

All colors can occur in different intensities, and the darkest hues are the most sought-after. Unfortunately, the color is not always evenly distributed, and this may not be noticeable until a stone is cut. A good diamond cutter can often remove the areas of poor color, and sometimes he is surprised to find a magnificent gem color inside what looked like an ugly stone.

You may wonder whether emerald green diamonds or ruby-colored ones are ever confused with real emeralds or rubies. There are many tests, even simple ones using X-rays or ultraviolet light, that will identify the stones. Besides, even to the inexperienced eye, no other gem sparkles quite like a diamond.

THE NOT-SO-PERFECT DIAMOND

In spite of expert cutting, some seemingly good stones will not exhibit the brilliance expected. If a stone is flawed, some of the light will be lost by absorption. Less than 20 percent of the stones mined each year are suitable for use as gems anyway. The rest become industrial diamonds.

External blemishes such as scratches, chips, nicks, or pits can be removed in the cutting process. Internal flaws such as cracks, inclusions, or bubbles are more serious. Inclusions, both dark and light, are various kinds of small crystals that were formed at the same time as the gem and were surrounded by their "host" because it grew more rapidly. Some of the things found inside diamonds are garnets, green olivine crystals, and even smaller diamonds.

Sometimes diamonds can be subjected to laser beams, which will burn out a black flaw and leave a barely visible hole. Usually small flaws, if not visible enough to affect the clarity of the cut gem, are considered of less importance than a poor color.

2.

REAL, FAKE, OR SYNTHETIC?

Through the years, jewelers and scientists have made many attempts to improve upon the appearance of diamonds. Before the eighteenth century, diamonds set in jewelry were backed by foil to intensify their brilliance or enhance their color. Sometimes a reflector of crystal glass was set behind the stone.

Jewelers also used an indelible pencil or ink to add a violet tone to the back of the gem. Just as mixing the light of complimentary colors can produce white light, the violet partly neutralized a stone's yellowish tinge. Such a change was only temporary and easily detected, but later methods of reducing the yellow were more refined and were noticeable only to an expert.

ARTIFICIALLY COLORED DIAMONDS

About 1904, a British scientist named William Crookes found that he could change off-color diamonds into a pleasing blue-green by exposing them to radium. This method was quickly abandoned, however, when it was discovered that the stones became radioactive. Even today, traces of radioactivity are still found in those old diamonds.

A new method to improve the color came about with the invention of the cyclotron in 1929. In this machine, the diamonds are irradiated by bombarding them with such things as alpha particles, protons, and deuterons. This moves the diamond atoms away from their regular position in the crystal, which changes the color. The preferred techique today is to bombard the stones with electrons or neutrons in a nuclear reactor. Both methods give essentially the same results, and in both cases the stones are radioactive for only a few hours after the treatment. It is impossible to know what color will result, because each diamond is different in structure and the length or intensity of the irradiation is not always the same.

Heating diamonds to temperatures of 700 to 900 degrees Centigrade after irradiation also results in various color changes. Probably the largest diamond to have been irradiated and heat treated was an unattractive yellowish 104.52-carat cut stone. The irradiation changed it into a deep green color, and the heating produced a gorgeous golden yellow color. Green is the most easily-produced hue by irradiation, and heating usually changes that into some shade of yellow or golden brown. It is difficult to get a good red, blue, or purple, and the much-admired rosy tint is nearly always natural. In some cases, scientists have even been able to turn an off-color yellow stone into a perfectly clear one.

Irradiated colored diamonds have been commercially

available since about 1950. Some buyers will always hold out for an untreated diamond, but artificially-colored ones are very popular. A few of these are easily detected by a jeweler, but most only by an expert gemologist using elaborate and expensive equipment.

It is almost impossible for a diamond to keep any secrets from an expert. In the early 1970s, an Israeli physicist, Samuel Shtrikman, discovered that each diamond is unique. When you shine a laser beam into the top facet of a cut diamond, it will send back its own special pattern of reflections, as distinctive as a fingerprint. Before this was known, there was no way to identify a gemstone. Police sometimes had to return stolen diamonds to a suspected thief, because they had no means of proving their true ownership.

FAKE DIAMONDS

There have been counterfeit diamonds almost as long as they have been the favorite gemstone. The most common fake is ordinary cut glass with a very thin reflective coating of silver or gold on the back.

In the eighteenth century, so-called "paste" diamonds were not only common but considered fashionable. They were made of a hard, brilliant glass containing lead oxide. Called *strass*, it was named after the Viennese jeweler, Josef Stras or Strass, who later became the court jeweler of King Louis XV of France. This colorless lead glass has a dispersive

WHICH DIAMOND IS THE FAKE?

It takes a gemologist with sophisticated equipment to positively identify some fake diamonds, but there are simple tests you can do that will reveal a few of the impostors. You should always have a real diamond to compare with the suspect stone.

Hold each stone horizontal and gradually tilt it away from you. The diamond will retain its brilliance while the light seems to fade from most imitations. The diamond has much higher thermal conductivity than other colorless gems, so it is colder to the touch and becomes warm more quickly. If you breathe on the two stones simultaneously, the mist will clear sooner from the diamond.

A small loose diamond can be picked up with a damp finger, but most simulants (imitators) will drop off immediately. Also, the electrical charge produced when a diamond is briskly rubbed will cause it to attract and hold small bits of paper. Furthermore, most diamond substitutes are more transparent than the real thing. It is possible to see newsprint through many of them, unless something was put on the back when they were mounted.

("fire"-producing) power that gives it a convincing appearance, and it is still used today. It cannot pass the hardness test, however; it scratches and rubs just from everyday use.

Larger diamonds have been faked by cementing two flat ones together or by affixing a thin layer of diamond to glass, and clear quartz crystals and colorless sapphires have often posed as diamonds. Manmade stones called Fabulite and Diamonaire, which closely resemble diamonds, were put on the market at one time. They are hard to find in jewelry stores today, but a few jewelers are still willing to order them.

One of the best diamond imitators is zircon, a mineral occurring in tetragonal (four-sided) crystals. It is found in several colors. The most common color is yellow-brown, and when that is heated, it turns first blue and then colorless. Just as the diamond does, it produces a lot of "fire," but it is very much softer.

JYNTHETIC DIAMONDJ

Unlike fake diamonds, the synthetic are the real thing. They have the same chemical composition as the natural diamonds but are produced in a laboratory instead of in the earth.

Ever since it became known, some 200 years ago, that diamond consists of nothing more than pure carbon, scientists have reasoned that it shouldn't be difficult to imitate the natural birth of the gem by subjecting carbonaceous material to extreme pressures and temperatures. Around 1880, a Scottish chemist named James Ballantyne Hannay produced what seemed to be small diamond crystals, but attempts to repeat his experiments were unsuccessful.

It was not until 1953 that a reliable way of making synthetic diamonds was found. A Swedish scientist named B. von Platen was the lucky experimenter. Unaware of his success, scientists at General Electric Company in Schenectady, New York, thought they were the first when they showed off their synthetic diamonds in February of 1955. Their method was similar to that used in Sweden: dissolving a form of carbon in molten metal and subjecting it to high temperatures and pressure. In the General Electric laboratory, experimenters used pressures of over 1.5 million pounds to a square inch and temperatures ranging from about 3,500 to 5,500 degrees Fahrenheit.

In 1959, the De Beers Company in South Africa announced that it, too, had a way to make synthetic diamonds, and it opened a factory near Johannesburg. Ireland began manufacturing synthetics in 1963, and soon several African nations, Japan, Czechoslovakia, and the USSR all had their diamond factories.

The first crystals produced were very small and dark in color and could be used only for industrial purposes. Also, they cost much more than the real thing. Now it is cheaper to manufacture than to mine, and these stones have several advantages over their natural counterparts. They can be manufactured in shapes needed for particular tasks and can be made into better conductors of heat—something important in our newest technologies.

Crystals of synthetic diamonds are generally more regular than natural ones. Using the lowest possible temperature and pressure usually produces cubes; raising both will give octahedra, with 8 sides. Dodecahedra (12-sided) rarely occur. Another difference is that on synthetic crystals the faces are smooth, whereas they are very rough on natural stones. Imperfections such as inclusions and fractures are found in manmade stones as well as in natural ones.

Variations in temperature and pressure also affect the color of the synthetics produced. Black is most common at the lower temperatures, and the color changes to shades of green, yellow, and other hues as the temperature is raised. Blue stones are produced, as in nature, by inclusions of boron as an impurity.

Producing gem-quality stones was not easy at first, because the extremely high pressure had to be maintained for longer than fifty hours at a time. In 1970 General Electric announced the "birth" of several fine quality stones, some weighing as much as one carat each. A diamond-cutter who worked with them said that during the cutting process they behaved no differently from natural stones. Three of these first synthetic gemstones—a clear crystal, a pale blue, and a canary yellow—were given to the Smithsonian Institution in Washington D.C. Synthetic diamonds of gem quality, being much harder to produce than the industrial ones, are much more expensive than real ones of the same size and quality. Because it is not profitable to manufacture them, synthetic diamonds will probably not be found in jewelry stores for quite awhile.

Industrial diamonds are produced by using several different techniques. It was found that a gas containing carbon could be used for growing the stone on small diamond "seeds." In 1988, a Japanese electrical engineer shocked the world by showing that he could make diamonds almost out of thin air by using an acetylene torch and a metal disk of molybdenum. Here in our own country, a high school student named Lea Potts succeeded in producing diamonds in her garage by using the same method.

Although General Electric and other companies making synthetics are interested mainly in meeting the great demand for industrial diamonds, some experimenting with gemstones is still going on. As they become easier to produce, their price should also go down. To most people, synthetic diamonds look just like the real thing, but they will never be held in the same high esteem as the great gems that have come from the world's mines. Can you imagine the British royalty, for example, being crowned with stones made in a laboratory?

3.

WHERE DO DIAMONDS COME FROM?

Whenever the origin of something is uncertain, people like to invent stories to explain it. Ancient man had several to explain where diamonds come from.

In the Sanskrit language the word for the stone was *vajra* (thunderbolt), because it was thought that they were created by lightning. In other cultures it was said that diamonds were splinters of stars fallen to Earth, or that they were dewdrops that hardened when the planets were close together in the sky. There was even a myth that the god of mines had pulverized other precious stones, such as rubies and sapphires, to form a new one that would give off all of their colors.

We will probably never know when diamonds were first discovered. Old documents show that they were known in India as early as the seventh century B.C. There are no records, however, that tell where they were found or how they were mined at that time.

VALLEY OF THE DIAMONDS

For hundreds of years, in ancient times, people talked

about a mysterious Valley of the Diamonds. It was first mentioned by Epiphanius (ca. 315-403 A.D.), bishop of Cyprus, and it also appears in the memoirs (ca. 500 A.D.) of Chinese princes of the Liang dynasties. It is a man known as the "pseudo-Aristotle," however, author of the oldest Arabic treatise on mineralogy (ca. 750 A.D.), who gives us the following story.

Alexander the Great, who according to history set out on a campaign through the mountains of India in 327 B.C., came upon this famous valley. He had heard that it was guarded by poisonous snakes, who could kill a man just by gazing at him. He and his men approached slowly, holding mirrors in front of them. The serpents were caught by the reflections of their own eyes and perished.

Though the men could see the diamonds, the valley was so deep and its sides so steep that they couldn't get to them. Alexander then ordered his men to slaughter some sheep and throw the carcasses into the valley. Before long, vultures appeared and began carrying away bits of the dead animals. The diamonds stuck to the flesh and were carried to the birds' nests. The men followed the birds and quickly retrieved the stones.

This story was probably kept alive by diamond merchants who wanted to keep the real source of their gems a secret. As fantastic as it sounds, there are certain elements of truth in the story. Diamonds do stick to grease, such as sheep fat. Vultures do seek animal carcasses, and all sorts of strange objects have been found in their nests.

Courtesy of Nona Maloney.

ANCIENT ΣOURCEΣ

One thing that is fairly certain is that all the early known diamonds were found in river beds. No one knows how long ago they were carried there by floods and sank to the bottom. In some desert regions, diamonds were found under the surface of the sand where rivers had dried up many thousands of years before.

Probably diamonds were discovered in India in ancient times during gold-mining operations, because the two minerals are found together in alluvial (riverbed) deposits. The ancient fortress city of Golconda, which lay in the area between the modern cities of Mumbai (Bombay) and Chennai (Madras), was the center of the diamond trade. Although records do not indicate where the early stones were mined, travelers saw alluvial mining taking place in that same part of India during the seventeenth century. For over two thousand years India was the only known source of diamonds. Its mines were almost depleted when another lucky discovery kept the European diamond cutters from going out of business.

DISCOVERIES IN BRAZIL

Diamonds are usually discovered in or on the ground, but you might say that they were once discovered in a poker game. In Brazil in the early 1700s, gold miners often amused themselves by playing gambling games with cards, using large pebbles from the stream bed as chips. In 1725 a newcomer, Sebastino Leme do Prado, who had spent some time in India, recognized some pebbles as diamond crystals. To the miners' surprise, he insisted on buying up all their chips.

He took the stones to Europe where diamond cutters pronounced them of equal quality to those found in India. This was not good news for diamond merchants. They knew that the only way to keep the price high on good gemstones was not to flood the market, so they didn't want to see a lot of stones coming from a new source. They began spreading rumors that the Brazilian stones were not real diamonds, or that they were of very poor quality. For many years, Brazil had to ship the gems to Goa in India (then a Portuguese colony) so they could be sold from there as Indian diamonds.

As soon as the gold prospectors found out what the pebbles really were, a horde of diamond-seekers rushed to the river beds. Brazil soon became the world's biggest supplier of the gemstones.

Although diamond mining never became a large-scale industry in Brazil, prospecting has never stopped, and many good gemstones have turned up. Of greatest importance during the last one hundred years has been the production there of a special black diamond called *carbonado*. The hardest known form of the stone, it is extremely valuable in industry.

The demand for gem-quality diamonds began to soar just as Brazil's output and the world's supply of rough diamonds was shrinking. European diamond cutters were on the point of having to close their shops when a lucky find in Africa rescued them.

EUREKA! WHAT A PEBBLE!

In 1866, the fifteen-year-old son of a Dutch Boer farmer in South Africa picked up a pretty pebble on the bank of the Orange River and brought it home for his sister to play with. A family friend, Mr. Van Niekerk, noticed it and thought that it might be of value. He wanted to buy it from the children's mother, but she insisted on giving it to him.

Diamond mining in Brazil in the late 1800s.

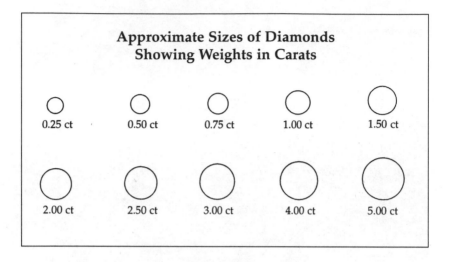

The first few people who looked at the stone claimed it was worthless. Then it was mailed to an amateur mineralogist for analysis. He and the experts he consulted declared it to be a diamond of 21.25 carats.

The word "carat" evolved from "carob." Early Indian merchants used the seeds of the carob tree on their scales to balance the diamonds, and their average weight was used as a standard until this century. We now have a "metric carat" which equals exactly 200 milligrams or $1/142$ of an ounce.

The large diamond found by the Boer boy was named "Eureka," and in London it was cut to a gem weighing 10.73 carats (about twenty times the size of the stone in an average engagement ring). After changing hands several times during the years, the diamond was returned to South Africa where it was put on display in the Houses of Parliament in Pretoria.

The Lichtenburg Rush in 1926. Although later than the first diamond finds, the scene is the same: thousands of stakeholders rush to stake out claims at this alluvial source. Courtesy of DeBeers.

THE GREAT
DIAMOND RUSH

Three years after the discovery of the first South African diamond, a shepherd found another interesting "pebble" in the same area. He took it to Van Niekerk and received five hundred sheep, ten oxen, and a horse for the 83.5-carat stone. The rough diamond was cut into a pear shape weighing 47.75 carats and was named the "Star of South Africa."

When this discovery became known, the great diamond rush began. By 1870 there were about ten thousand claims along the Orange and Vaal rivers. Every week hundreds of new faces appeared and more sprawling tent towns of prospectors were set up.

In July of that year, an oxcart driver showed off a large diamond which he said he had found on a farm about 60 miles from the Vaal diggings. No one would believe him, because everyone thought that diamonds could be found only in river beds. Not long afterward, on another farm in that area, someone noticed diamonds embedded in the walls of the house. The owner had made his mortar out of the diamond-bearing soil on his property.

Prospectors now decided to leave the rivers to try their luck in the "dry diggings." New waves of hopeful miners arrived from many parts of the world, and as the mining camps grew they merged to form a town which was named Kimberley.

THE BLUE GROUND

Diamonds in the new area were found in a very different type of soil from the river gravel. Underneath the loose surface dirt in which the men found the first stones was a yellow clay that was even richer in diamonds. Soon miners discovered that the areas of yellow clay were enclosed in a sort of

The Formation of a Kimberlite Pipe

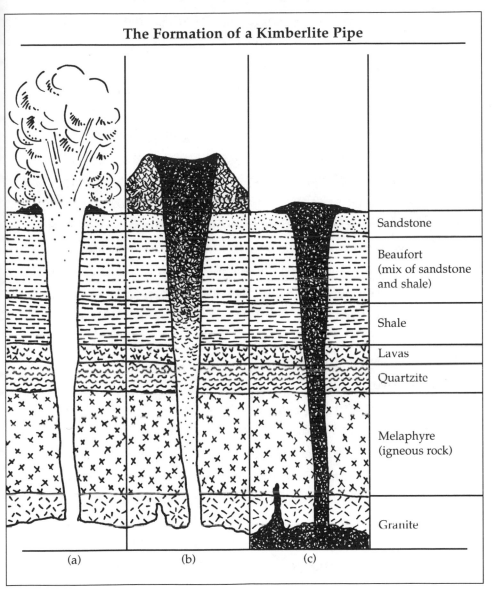

	Sandstone
	Beaufort (mix of sandstone and shale)
	Shale
	Lavas
	Quartzite
	Melaphyre (igneous rock)
	Granite

(a)   (b)   (c)

The molten magma in which the diamonds were formed was exploded to the surface (a) and cooled into a rock called kimberlite. The cone it formed (b) was eroded by rain and wind (c), which washed the diamonds into nearby rivers.

pit, which was later called a pipe. Geologists felt certain that all the diamonds that had been found in the river beds had originated in these pipes of yellow clay.

As the miners dug through this layer, the clay changed gradually into a hard blue ground called kimberlite, which also contained diamonds. The yellow ground had originally been blue kimberlite but weathered as it became exposed to surface water and air.

But what were these kimberlite pipes that seemed to be the original source of diamonds? Carrot-shaped, they kept getting narrower as they went down into the earth. Although pipes have been mined to several thousand feet, it is not known how deep each one goes. It has been estimated that some may go as far as 53 miles toward the center of the earth.

Of the nearly one thousand pipes discovered in southern Africa, the openings varied from about 6½ feet in diameter to over 4,000 feet. Some of these oval-shaped openings were level with the ground surface. Some projected above, and others had weathered into shallow depressions.

For a while it was thought that the pipes were the throats of extinct volcanoes and that the blue ground was solidified lava, but that was incorrect. There is no evidence that the sides of the pipes were ever tremendously hot and no sign of lava flows in the vicinity. It seemed that neither the yellow nor the blue ground was the primary source of diamonds after all.

Geologists now know that the stones were formed at depths of 80 to 120 miles in the uppermost part of the Earth's mantle—the 1,800-mile-thick region that lies between the molten inner core and the solid rocky crust. Intense heat and pressure changed carbon into diamond crystals, and the explosive pressure of gasses shot them to the surface in masses of kimberlite.

In 1983, a geochemist at the Massachusetts Institute of Technology succeeded in determining the age of diamonds. He crushed over a thousand stones to free the garnet impurities, because unlike pure diamond, garnet contains radioactive isotopes whose rate of decay reveals its age. The garnets, and thus the diamonds, turned out to be 3.3 billion years old.

Kimberlite is a fragmented igneous (fire-produced) rock containing many minerals such as corundum, chromium, quartz, and zircon. The composition varies from mine to mine, sometimes even within a single pipe. Many kimberlite pipes contain no diamonds at all.

All kimberlite is easily decomposed by weathering. Erosion is always going on, and it was much more violent millions of years ago. Torrential rains would quickly have washed away the blue ground, which probably had been thrust up 3,000 or 4,000 feet above the surrounding surface.

Diamond-bearing pipes have never been found in India or Brazil in spite of much searching by geologists. In fact, they are found in only a few countries of the world, most of them on the African continent. Of all the diamonds mined, about 80 percent have come from alluvial deposits in river beds. In general, they produce the best gemstones, because only the finest crystals are able to withstand the rough journey and continual buffeting of water.

WORLD DIAMOND PRODUCTION *(Million metric carats)*					
1975		**1980**		**1997**	
The Congo	17.00	USSR	10.85	Australia	19.20
USSR	12.00	The Congo	10.23	The Congo	19.00
South Africa	7.80	South Africa	8.50	Botswana	12.00
Botswana	2.37	Botswana	5.10	Russia	8.00
Ghana	2.25	Namibia	1.56	South Africa	4.30

Figure 1

AROUND THE GLOBE

During the twentieth century diamonds have been found in many African countries. The biggest producers have been Angola, Botswana, Central African Republic, Ghana, Ivory Coast, Namibia, Sierra Leone, South Africa, and The Congo (formerly Zaire). Several of these nations produce only industrial diamonds, however; nothing of gem quality.

Diamonds of good quality have been mined in Guyana and Venezuela in South America. There are known deposits in Australia, Borneo, Canada, China, Java, the Malay Peninsula, Russia, Sumatra, and Thailand, but only a few (except for those in Australia and Russia) have proved worth exploiting. Canada, however, is believed to be a potential big producer. Though there is still some mining in India, the output is only a trickle compared to what it was in the past.

For several decades about 95 percent of all the world's diamonds came from Africa. In the 1950s Russia began large-scale alluvial mining, mostly in Siberia. By the late 1970s over 300 kimberlite pipes had been discovered, and Russia's output was soon about equal to that of the two largest-producing African countries, The Congo and South Africa. During the 1980s it was pushed out of first place on the list of world producers by Australia, which is still the biggest diamond producer today. Australia also produces some rare fancies of a beautiful pink color.

DIAMOND FINDJ IN THE UNITED JTATEJ

Diamonds are not nearly as rare as most people think. Many have been found right here in our own country. Finds from twenty-two different states have been authenticated, as noted in figure 2, and there may be others that haven't been publicized yet. Most of the discoveries have occurred in three areas: the foothills of the Sierra Nevada range in California; along the eastern base of the Allegheny Mountains (between Virginia and Georgia); and in the Great Lakes region (from Wisconsin to Ohio).

Stones are most often found by people panning for gold. Over five hundred were found in California during the great gold rush, which began in 1848. Though the source of these or the alluvial deposits in the Alleghenies is not certain, those

AUTHENTICATED DIAMOND FINDS
IN THE UNITED STATES (Counties)*

Alabama: Lee, Shelby, St. Clair

Arkansas: Pike, White

California: Amador, Butte, El Dorado, Del Norte, Humboldt, Imperial, Placer, Nevada, Plumas, Trinity, Tulare, Tuolemne

Colorado: Moffat

Georgia: Burke, Camden, Clayton, Hall, Lee, Twiggs, White

Idaho: Adams

Illinois: Jefferson, Jersey, McDonough, Washington

Indiana: Brown, Morgan

Kentucky: Adair

Louisiana: Bossier, Webster

Michigan: Cass, Dickinson, Iron, Menominee

Montana: Beaverhead, Deer Lodge

North Carolina: Burke, Cleveland, Lincoln, McDowell, Mecklenburg, Rutherford

Ohio: Clermont, Columbiana, Cuyahoga, Hamilton, Mahoning, Summit

Oregon: Curry, Josephine

Tennessee: DeKalb, Monroe, Roane, Union

Texas: Foard

Virginia: Chesterfield, Orange, Rockbridge, Spotsylvania, Tazewell

Washington: Skamania and various beaches along the coast

West Virginia: Monroe

Wisconsin: Dane, Kenosha, Langlade, Manitowoc, Milwaukee, Ozaukee, Pierce, Racine, Washington, Waukesha

Wyoming: Albany, Carbon, Campbell

Figure 2

found in stream beds in the Great Lakes region were brought down from Canada by glaciers during the Ice Age.

Except for a recent discovery in the Rocky Mountains of Colorado, the blue ground called kimberlite is found in only a few places in our country, mainly in Arkansas and Michigan. A pipe discovered near Murfreesboro, Arkansas, in 1906 has yielded more than seventy thousand diamonds, including the 40.23-carat "Uncle Sam"—the largest one found in this country to date. The area was actively mined until 1919 but is now part of Arkansas's Crater of Diamonds State Park. Visitors may dig there for a small fee and are allowed to keep any stones they find.

Probably the best-known gemstone unearthed at the state park is the Star of Arkansas, a white 15.33-carat diamond. It was found by a tourist, Mrs. A.L. Parker of Dallas, in 1956. After being cut into a flawless 8.27-carat gem, it brought $145,000 at an auction at Christie's in New York. Hillary Rodham Clinton wore a gold ring with a 4.25 dia-

---

Opposite: Almost all of these diamonds have been found in stream beds or gravel pits. Although kimberlite pipes have been found in the Great Lakes area, only a few insignificant diamonds have been found there. In the kimberlite pipes of Arkansas, however, more than 55,000 diamonds have been discovered.

For more detailed information on areas, write to the Geological Surveys of Alabama, Colorado, Georgia, Idaho, Illinois, Indiana, Kentucky, Michigan, Montana, North Carolina, Ohio, West Virginia, Wisconsin, Wyoming, or to the Arkansas Geological Commission, the California Division of Mines and Geology, the Montana Bureau of Mines and Geology, the Oregon Department of Geology and Mineral Industries, the Tennessee Division of Geology, the Texas Bureau of Economic Geology, the Virginia Division of Mineral Resources, or the Washington Department of Natural Resources.

Tourists searching the 35-acre collecting area at Crater of Diamonds State Park. Courtesy of the Arkansas Geological Commission.

mond crystal from the Crater of Diamonds during the 1992 Presidential Inaugural Ball in Washington, D.C.

In several states, good-sized diamonds were found by people just walking around. One "pebble" picked up in West Virginia in 1928 lay on a shelf for fifteen years until it was found to be a 32.25-carat diamond.

It was probably the knowledge that diamonds had been found by miners panning for gold that led to the greatest diamond hoax in history. In the fall of 1871, two rustic miners named Philip Arnold and John Slack entered San Francisco's Bank of California and asked to have the two heavy bags they were carrying placed in the bank's vault. A bank official was worried that it was loot taken in a stagecoach robbery, so the miners had to empty the bags on his desk. Out rolled sparkling diamonds and other gemstones that they said they had found while prospecting for gold. They added that there were lots more where these came from.

The bank's owner, multimillionaire William C. Ralston, became interested and offered them $300,000 for a half interest in their discovery. They refused to give him the location of their find, but they finally agreed to take two of Ralston's representatives, a businessman and a mining expert, to the diamond fields blindfolded. The representatives came back saying there was no doubt of either the genuineness of the stones or their rich potential.

The miners presented Ralston with still another bag of diamonds, some larger than dice. One of them, a 103-carat gem, was valued at $95,000 by a jeweler in San Francisco. To be absolutely certain of their worth, Ralston had the stones taken to New York to be evaluated by Tiffany and Company, the most reliable appraisers in the country. The report read: "These are beyond question precious stones of enormous value," and the big diamond was appraised as worth $150,000. Twenty-five San Francisco businessmen bought $2 million worth of stock and bought out Arnold and Slack for another $300,000.

Soon afterward a geologist, Clarence King, who was doing a survey for the United States government in a remote area of Colorado, stumbled upon the "diamond fields" and found that they had been salted with cheap diamonds and quartz crystals. He found places where someone had made a hole with a crowbar, dropped in a diamond and then tamped it shut. Because the salting had been done a year or two earlier, the heavy rains, wind, and snow had done a good job of removing the traces.

Needless to say, Ralston's new mining company was dissolved, and he paid back every dollar of his friends' $2 million investments.

NEW DIAMOND SOURCES

A few years ago, diamonds were discovered in lamproite, another igneous rock very much like kimberlite and also formed at great depths. The best-known deposit of this is at Argyle, in Western Australia, where mining was begun almost immediately.

Surprisingly, natural diamonds are sometimes formed in places other than deep below the Earth's crust. They have been found in meteorites and in the famous Meteor Crater, southeast of Flagstaff, Arizona. Scientists know that they were produced by some catastrophic event, but they cannot agree upon whether it happened on impact with Earth or somewhere in space.

To complicate matters, astronomers now believe that some stars may actually be diamonds. In 1998, Iowa State University professor Steve Kawaler wrote that it is believed that a pulsating star named BPM37093, which is about 17 light-years from Earth, is made up of carbon and oxygen in a crystallized state. Of a pale blue-green color, it could be considered an off-color diamond. This star is what is known as a white dwarf: the cooling remains of a star that was originally larger than our sun. Astronomers estimate that this "gemstone" weighs trillions of carats.

In March of 1996, physicist Tyrone Daulton of the Argonne National Laboratory in Illinois found diamonds in a hunk of uranium-rich coal that had never felt the heat of the Earth's mantle. He explained that when the uranium atoms inside the coal slammed into the carbon atoms, they disrupted their chemical bonds. New bonds were formed, some of them diamonds. Like those found in meteorites, these were too small to be of commercial value. One scientist jokingly said, "One might make a good engagement ring for an ant."

People will probably be hunting for diamonds as long as there is any earth left unturned. In spite of new finds, however, the supply will have to run out eventually. Nature does not provide unlimited reservoirs.

4.

MINING DIAMONDS

The first step in any kind of mining is deciding where to work. The early diamond prospector was usually an independent adventurer who stopped to dig in any area that looked promising. He had to learn not only what kind of gravel or soil holds diamonds, but how to tell the stone from similar ones found in the same area.

Not all rough diamonds look alike. In general, diamonds from alluvial deposits are much shinier than those found in kimberlite. In South America, however, stones found in one stream bed were described as "clear as dew" while those in a nearby river were called "creamy frosted." From ancient times until the beginning of the twentieth century, prospecting was largely a matter of trial and error.

RIVER DIGGINGS

Once a productive area was found, it was divided into separate claims. Along the rivers in South Africa each prospector worked his own bit of land.

Alluvial mining for diamonds was the same as for gold, and it has changed very little through the centuries. The miner

36

dug up river gravel with a shovel and put it through a series of sieves. The first one had a large mesh that retained only pebbles an inch or more in diameter. Few diamonds were that large, and they could easily be seen and picked out before the material was thrown away. The second sieve was finer and got rid of the sand, leaving the pebbles most likely to contain good diamonds. Any diamonds that passed through were too small to be worth recovering. Finally, the material was washed in the river in the third and smallest-meshed sieve to remove any remaining fine silt and expose the diamonds.

This process took a lot of time, and there were many days in which no diamonds at all turned up. Different contraptions developed by gold miners, such as the Long Tom and the Cradle, made it possible to handle larger quantities of gravel at a time. When diamond mining evolved from the lone prospector to the small company stage, dredges were used to speed up the work.

There was a unique method of recovery used in Brazil at one time. Finding that diamonds were sometimes trapped under boulders in the bottom of large rivers, miners used crude diving bells to go down and search for them.

DRY DIGGINGS

When diggers in South Africa left the rivers in 1871 and went to the new fields near the present city of Kimberley, they each staked out a claim as they had done at the river diggings. During the first rush to the two farms on which diamonds

The Kimberley Mine in the 1880s. The ropes crisscrossing from the rim on the kimberlite pipe run to thousands of individual claims below. Courtesy of De Beers.

were found, about six thousand claims were staked. These changed hands frequently. Sometimes a big price was paid for soil that turned out to be worthless, and sometimes a claim that seemed unproductive was given away and the following day turned out to be a bonanza.

At first only the surface soil was worked, but after the rich yellow ground below was found, the digging went much deeper. Owners of each claim had to contribute a 7½-foot strip of land to be used for roads so the ore could be taken out by oxcart.

As the pits got deeper, the operation became too costly for some of the miners. Cecil Rhodes, a British administrator in South Africa, began buying up the claims and entered into partnerships with owners who didn't want to sell out entirely.

By 1872, the roads that separated the claims had become unsafe. Some of the pits were dug with almost vertical sides, and weather conditions were eroding the yellow ground. Sometimes a whole team of oxen and its load would pitch headlong into a pit. Without the roads, miners had to stretch cables from the rim of the diggings to the claims below, and buckets of ore were drawn up by African workers operating windlasses.

When diggers reached a depth of about 80 feet, they found that instead of yellow ground there was now a blue and very hard layer. Miners became discouraged, partly because they assumed the supply of diamonds was running out and partly because the world economic depression in 1873 was making it almost impossible for them to find buyers for their stones.

THE BIG COMPANIES

Miners could hardly believe it when Cecil Rhodes and Barney Barnato, another newcomer to South Africa, continued buying up the worthless blue ground. But these two men had heard geologists say that the hard rock probably contained diamonds too. It turned out to be true. The two men quickly gained control of the Kimberley and De Beers mines and became exceedingly rich.

Cecil Rhodes, founder of De Beers, 1888. Courtesy of De Beers.

Diamond mining had once been close-to-the-surface work, but now it was necessary to sink shafts and dig tunnels. Only a big company could afford to do the work. Eventually the hard blue ground was honeycombed with chambers and their connecting tunnels. Tracks were laid for the tram cars that transported the ore.

By 1887 there were only three mining operations in the area: Kimberley (Barnato's company), De Beers (controlled by Rhodes), and a French company. Within a year, Rhodes bought out the French company, and Kimberley was liquidated and joined his De Beers Consolidated Mines Limited. By 1889, De Beers held a monopoly over the diamond industry.

Cecil Rhodes is remembered for two things besides his

diamond interests. The country of Southern Rhodesia (now Zimbabwe) was named for him, as was Northern Rhodesia (now Zambia). When Rhodes died in 1902, he left most of his immense fortune to provide support for carefully selected college graduates to attend Oxford University in England on Rhodes Scholarships.

MINING THE KIMBERLITE

Extracting the diamonds from the yellow ground had been comparatively easy. Shovels were used to pulverize the larger lumps, and then the soil was put through sieves as in the riverbed operations. What passed through was thrown away, and the remainder went to the picking tables.

Miners were unable to break up the hard blue ground with shovels, but they noticed that when it was exposed to air for a while it began to break up by itself. The ore was spread out on the ground and left to weather for three to six months.

The deeper the level from which the blue ground came, the longer it took to disintegrate. When it became necessary to leave the ore exposed for over a year, African workers were hired to break it up with picks and hammers. These people were virtual prisoners. They lived in a guarded compound for periods of six months or more and were not permitted to leave the mine during that time. When they were through working there, they were thoroughly searched and even X-rayed to see if they had stolen any diamonds by swallowing them.

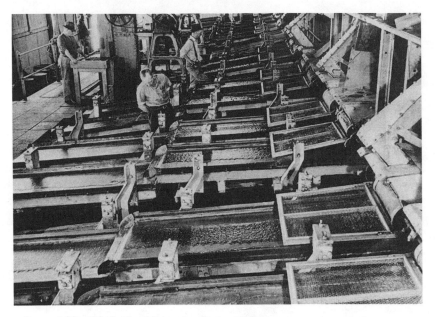

Grease tables, Kimberley Mines. Courtesy of De Beers.

Today the kimberlite is usually broken up underground. The chunks, which are extracted by blasting or heavy machinery, are shoveled into huge crushers. Though this is a highly efficient method, there is always the danger that a large diamond might be ruined.

Originally the diamonds were picked out of the crushed ore by hand. With the invention of the grease table, this process went much faster. The crushed blue ground was dumped onto sloping tables coated with a thick layer of grease and then washed with streams of water. Just as in the legend about Alexander and the Valley of Diamonds, the diamonds stuck to the grease. Everything else was washed away, and the diamond layer was scraped off and dropped into boiling water to melt the grease. Grease belts have since replaced the grease tables, but the method used is exactly the same.

MODERN METHOD♪ OF RECOVERY

Though basically the same, mining methods differ slightly from country to country, and from mine to mine within a country, because of the differences in the ground itself. As you might expect, Siberia is the most difficult area to mine. There the soil is permanently frozen to as deep as a thousand feet. Winter temperatures can go down as low as -90 degrees Fahrenheit, and only the top three to six feet thaw in summer. To get at the kimberlite, early miners first used high-pressure steam hoses to thaw the ground. Now, jet engines are placed where they want to dig, and the heat from the exhaust is piped directly to specially adapted drills. After the kimberlite is broken up by steam shovels, it goes to the treatment plant to have the diamonds extracted.

The grease table technique could not be used in Siberia, because water turns to ice in just seconds. The Russians developed the X-ray technique, which has been copied by many of the African mines. The X-ray identifies the diamonds by their fluorescence and separates them from the debris.

Throughout Africa there are many large treatment plants for handling both the kimberlite and alluvial gravel. Though diamonds are still extracted by earlier techniques us-

Final diamond sorting is still done by hand. Courtesy of Diamond Information Center on behalf of De Beers.

ing sieves and grease tables or belts, modern plants have many newer ways of recovery.

Some plants use electrostatic separators. Most diamonds are electrical insulators. When gravel is poured past positively-charged rollers, the diamonds will fall straight through, and the rest of the ore will be attracted to the rollers and diverted elsewhere.

In an optical separator, the material passes under a beam

of light in the dark. A diamond will reflect this light, and that activates a photocell which opens a gate through which the diamond drops. Besides the separators that use the X-ray technique developed by the Russians, there are those that use ultraviolet light, hydrochloric acid, or other chemicals.

Whatever method is used, before the diamonds can be sold they must go through machines that sort them according to size, shape, and color. The final sorting,which determines the quality and sale prices of the diamonds, must be done by hand by highly-trained individuals.

MODERN PROSPECTING

The deeper a kimberlite pipe is mined, the smaller the yield and the average size of the stones. Mines have to be abandoned when it is no longer profitable to work them. Even the best ore seldom produces as much as three carats of diamonds to the ton. So, prospecting must go on.

Because of the high cost, most research today is focused on known areas of kimberlite. Teams of university-trained geologists with modern equipment have replaced the solitary prospectors, and they are searching not for diamonds but for areas of possible kimberlite.

At times the yellow ground can be found easily. It holds more moisture than the surrounding soil and thus has more vegetation. Sometimes this can be seen only from the air. Photographs are taken at different altitudes from helicopters, planes, and even a space satellite. Different types of film, such as panchromatic and infrared, help in locating subterranean cracks that indicate the presence of kimberlite. Radar images obtained from planes can do the same. Radar has an advantage in that it can see through clouds, and images can be taken even at night.

Ground crews make maps of the magnetic fields in different localities to learn the nature of the rocks under the soil. Geologists obtain much the same information by studying the electric currents produced between electrodes placed in the soil at fixed intervals. Alluvial prospecting, as well as a search for kimberlite, is still going on in Africa, too. Huge drills that can go down almost 100 feet bring up samples of the ground below. Beaches along the west coast, near the mouths of rivers, have been found to contain large diamond deposits 30 to 60 feet below the sand.

At the present, mining is also being done under the ocean. If you live near the coast, however, don't get your hopes up about digging for diamonds. It costs thousands of dollars a day to rent one of the offshore drilling rigs needed for bringing them up.

The large mining companies are always out there looking for new areas, but they try to keep their efforts as inconspicuous as possible. No one can predict where the next important discovery is likely to occur. Wouldn't it be exciting if something spectacular turned up in our own country some day?

5.

FROM PEBBLE TO GEMSTONE

The term "lapidary" refers to someone who works with all kinds of precious and semiprecious stones, but the one who specializes in diamonds is usually called a "diamond cutter." Though the gemstone cannot really be cut by a knife, the process of removing any part of it is called "diamond cutting." Sometimes the word "fashioning" is used instead. It covers all the stages of craftsmanship that lead from a rough diamond to a gem ready for setting.

It is uncertain whether diamond cutting originated in India or in Europe. The art remained a trade secret for several centuries, partly due to the belief that tampering with this stone would destroy its magical powers.

BRUTING

The first written account of diamond cutting in Europe is from 1568. An Italian, Benvenuto Cellini, described what is known today as "bruting." The stone was shaped merely by rubbing one diamond with another by hand. In spite of the leather gloves they wore, the workers' hands became swollen and sore. Relief came with the development of the grinding wheel in the 1660s. The iron edge of the wheel was treated with a mixture of diamond powder and oil, and the diamond powder was as good an abrasive as another diamond.

Working with diamonds was a handicraft industry usually done in the home, and the secrets of the trade were passed down from father to son. At first the wheel was powered by hand by the women in the family. In 1822 artisans began to use horse power. Before the end of the century, steam engines were turning the wheels. The twentieth century brought electric motors.

For a long time, the size of the diamond was more important than its brilliance. As much of the original stone as possible was retained. This meant either keeping the shape of the crystal itself or choosing a new shape that wouldn't require much bruting.

It first became fashionable to change the shape of the natural crystal around the beginning of the fourteenth century, when the top point was ground off leaving a flat surface called the "table."

Around 1641 the Mazarin cut became popular. Named after Cardinal Mazarin of France, it was octagonal in shape and had slanted facets both above and below the girdle, or center, of the stone. This was closely followed by the rose cut, which was flat at the base and had facets cut like the opening petals of a rose on top. Because it wasn't designed to bend light up from the bottom of the stone, it lacked the brillance seen in more modern cuts and is rarely used today.

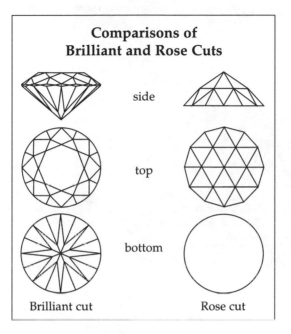

Comparisons of
Brilliant and Rose Cuts

side

top

bottom

Brilliant cut   Rose cut

CLEAVING

An octahedron is not the easiest shape to prepare for setting in jewelry, and bruting took a lot of time, so diamond cutters began cutting the crystal by a process called "cleaving." This was already being used in the fashioning of other gemstones.

A diamond can be split in the same way as a piece of wood—with a wedge and a mallet—because it, too, has a natural grain. It can be divided in any one of four directions as long as it is done precisely along a cleavage plane. If not, the diamond will shatter.

Although cleaving was the first step in the cutting process, it was not taken without preliminary study of the crystal. Each diamond is different, and its inclusions and

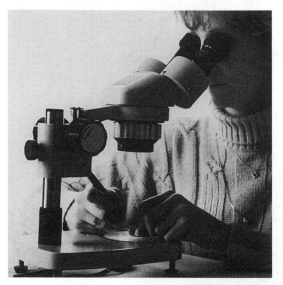

Marking a diamond for cutting. Courtesy of the Diamond Information Center on behalf of De Beers.

Cutting a diamond by machine. Courtesy of the Diamond Information Center on behalf of De Beers.

other imperfections as well as the cleavage planes have to be located before a final shape can be selected. Experts have often studied a diamond for many months before deciding where to make the first cut.

Polishing a diamond is done today by machine.
Courtesy of the Diamond Information Center on behalf of De Beers.

The technique of cleaving, still used for some diamonds today, has not changed at all through the centuries. Once a cleavage plane is found, a small notch is made in it. A wedge or a rather thick, unsharpened knife blade is placed in the notch and given a sharp tap with a mallet. This operation has been rapidly disappearing and is used today mainly for splitting very large stones or removing flawed portions of a crystal.

SAWING

A saw for cutting gemstones appeared in the nineteenth century. It wasn't very effective, however, on the hard diamond crystal. It took from eight to ten months to saw through a large stone. In about 1900 a saw specifically for diamonds was patented. The circular blade, which is 3 to 4 inches in diameter and of paper-thin bronze, is charged with diamond dust and continues to recharge itself with bits of the crystal being cut. Though the blade revolves at speeds from 4,500 to 6,500 revolutions per minute, it still takes a few hours to saw through a one-carat rough diamond.

Sawing is preferable to cleaving, because a diamond can be cut in any direction without regard to cleavage planes. Besides being faster and less dangerous to the gem, it is a more economical procedure.

Now a new laser saw is rapidly replacing the bronze saw. Though it shortens the cutting time, it is more expensive and the diamond loss is greater than with the bronze saw. By the time a gem is finished, it has lost from 50 to 60 percent of its original weight—but it has increased greatly in value.

FINIJHING THE DIAMOND

In a typical diamond factory the stone passes through many hands, all of them expert. From the cleaver or sawyer, it goes to a person known as a girdler. Using a lathe, this worker smoothes the stone until it is roughly beet-shaped.

Now a lapper, or blocker, whose specialty is opening up the first facets, takes over. The angle and size of each facet must not vary even the smallest fraction of an inch from the standard, or the value of the finished gem will go down. The

Popular Diamond Cuts

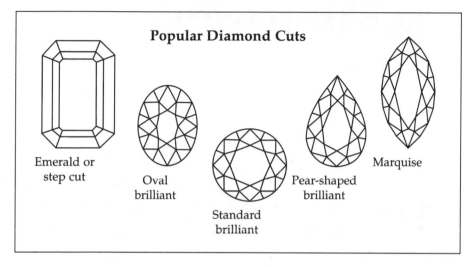

Emerald or
step cut

Oval
brilliant

Standard
brilliant

Pear-shaped
brilliant

Marquise

last person to work on the diamond is the brillianteer, who cuts and polishes the remaining facets.

Early in the twentieth century, physicists figured out exactly what proportions and angles were necessary to achieve the maximum brilliance. The new shape, quite appropriately called the brilliant cut, is a round stone of fifty eight facets. It is flat on top, widens a bit with sloping facets, then narrows, coming to a sharp point at the back. It looks a bit like the old-fashioned rose cut turned upside down. This faceted stone can be adapted to almost any shape. The most popular variations are the pear shape, heart shape, oval, and a pointed oval called the marquise cut.

Machines now do many of the jobs in diamond fashioning automatically, but for a really fine stone there must be a skilled hand guiding the machine.

6.

ADORNED WITH DIAMONDS

People have been fascinated with gemstones from earliest times. Archaeologists have found necklaces of garnet, turquoise, and other gems, plus elaborate pieces of jewelry set with colored stones, dating back as far as 2,500 years B.C. The early history of diamonds, however, is pretty much shrouded in mystery.

NOT FOR SHOW AT FIRST

Historians believe that when diamonds were first discovered in India they were valued not as objects of adornment but for certain magical powers attributed to them.

In its natural state, or even with a bit of polishing, the gemstone was not very beautiful. It was a long time before the diamond became the dominant jewel and beautiful stone that it is today. In many of the early civilizations, pearls were number one in popularity. In Europe during most of the Middle Ages, diamonds ranked behind rubies and emeralds as well as pearls.

Their unattractiveness wasn't the only thing responsible for the lack of interest in them. Very few diamonds ever reached Europe. All stones over 10 carats that were found in India belonged to the local rulers there, and the Arabs and Persians traded for the rest. It was not until after the knights returned from the last of their Crusades to the Holy Land (1095-1272) that diamonds, which they brought with them, became known in Europe.

ONLY FOR ROYALTY

During the Middle Ages, only the rulers in Europe owned diamonds, and only a few did at that. We know from his will that in 1308 the Duke of Anjou owned eight polished diamonds set in gold. In the inventory of the possessions of King Charles V of France drawn up in 1379, only one diamond is mentioned. Most early inventories on record do not even mention the stones.

Before the year 1400, precious stones in royal treasuries were not used much for personal adornment. They were used mainly as security for loans to raise armies and fight wars. The earliest known painting of a monarch wearing jewels is of Henry IV of England, painted in the early 1400s. On each sleeve he was wearing a splendid octahedron of a beautiful blue color, presumably a diamond.

It was not only hard to acquire a diamond but illegal in many cases. In Spain there were laws forbidding anyone but a reigning monarch and the next in line to the throne to own gold, silver, or precious stones. France and England had similar laws. It wasn't until nearly the end of the fifteenth century that knights in England were allowed to own precious gems. At a jousting tournament held in 1494, King Henry VII of England rewarded the most skilled knight with a diamond ring.

When trading ships finally began arriving with quantities of Indian diamonds, all the rulers of Europe started collecting them. Then, when the new art of diamond cutting revealed the sparkle of the gems, they were worn in great profusion, not only in jewelry but on clothing. They were sewed onto the sleeves and the trains of royal robes. Hats, shoes, buttons, belts, and belt buckles were adorned with them. They were even set into watch cases, snuff boxes, and drinking cups.

King Louis XIV of France (1638-1715) was the first of the "big spenders." He bought thousands of carats of diamonds, and they decorated almost every article of clothing he wore, from head to toe. He even gave them to lesser rulers whose respect he wished to gain. Louis XVI, who ascended the throne about one hundred years later, was an even greater diamond lover. He not only wore them himself but showered his queen, Marie Antoinette, with elaborate pieces of diamond jewelry.

NOT FOR THE LADIES AT FIRST

Before and during the early Middle Ages the diamond, because of its durability, was the symbol of fearlessness and

Agnes Sorel

strength. Kings had the stone set in the hilts of their swords, and it is natural that they would be the first to wear them.

King Louis IX of France (1214-1270) issued a royal decree forbidding women, even princesses, to wear diamonds. This pious ruler, who later was canonized by the Roman Catholic Church as Saint Louis, felt that the only woman worthy of wearing diamonds was the Holy Virgin herself. For a while, the set stones were used only to adorn objects in churches and other religious establishments.

The first woman in France known to have disobeyed the royal order wasn't even of noble blood. Agnes Sorel, a court beauty eager to become the favorite of King Charles VII, suddenly appeared one day in 1444 wearing an elegant diamond necklace. The courtiers stared open-mouthed. They were certain that the king would punish this woman for her audacity. Instead, Agnes became his favorite as she had planned, and soon after this the diamond changed from being a royal symbol of power and wealth to one of feminine adornment.

When diamonds became accessible to anyone who could afford them, the crystals were often set in rings with the point of one of the two pyramids toward the front. During the reign of Queen Elizabeth I of England (1558-1603), it was the fad for lovers to use them for scribbling messages or poems on window panes. It is claimed that the queen herself exchanged rhymes this way with Sir Walter Raleigh.

THE QUEEN'S NECKLACE

The most famous jewels in the history of the western world were those in an extravagant necklace said to belong to Marie Antoinette. Although she never owned the necklace, many historians claim that the scandal surrounding it was the spark that started the French Revolution in 1789 and thus led to the beheading of her husband Louis XVI and herself, and the disgrace of a respected cardinal.

The necklace was actually made with the idea of selling it to Louis XV for his court favorite, Madame Du Barry. When the court jewelers showed her their design, for which they had spent two years collecting the flawless stones, she wholeheartedly approved. Unfortunately, King Louis died of smallpox before the necklace could be completed.

The jewelers decided to finish the necklace anyway. It was breathtaking, composed of 647 diamonds whose weight totaled almost 3,000 carats. Even the "smallest" diamonds weighed over four carats apiece. An appraiser at that time set its value at $500,000; today it would be worth over $6 million.

Believing that King Louis XVI would want it for his queen, Marie Antoinette, the jewelers offered it to him. As he felt she already had enough extravagant pieces of jewelry, he turned down the offer. The jewelers couldn't think of anyone in Europe who could afford their asking price of 1,800,000 francs. When the queen's first child was born, they hoped that Louis would want to celebrate the big event by giving her the necklace. They thought that if they showed it to the queen, she would certainly beg for it. Imagine their shock when she told them that for that amount of money, France could buy a badly needed warship.

The jewelers next approached the Countess de la Motte, who was said to be a friend of the queen. They promised her a commission of 200,000 francs if she could get the queen to change her mind. She hatched a scheme by which she expected to get the necklace as well as her commission.

First she contacted Cardinal Rohan, who needed the queen's backing to become prime minister, but who could never get an audience with her. She told him that the queen wanted the diamond necklace badly enough to buy it for herself, but she didn't want her husband to know about it. If the good cardinal would buy it for her, the queen would repay him in installments that Louis wouldn't be apt to notice. The cardinal felt that this might lead to the appointment he wanted so badly.

Cardinal Rohan signed the contract with the jewelers, agreeing to pay 1,600,000 francs down and 400,000 francs plus interest every six months. He was given the necklace, which he took to the countess, who had a supposedly trusted courier ready to take it to the queen.

As soon as he left, so did the countess and her husband—for England, along with her 200,000 franc commission and the necklace. Once there, they hacked the necklace to pieces and sold the diamonds. The count and countess spent their money as fast as they got it. She had a luxurious carriage with six horses, whose harnesses were adorned with diamonds and topazes. He wore both emerald and ruby rings on each finger.

They sent the money for the first installment on the necklace to the cardinal, but when the time for the second installment came around, there was no money left. The jewelers naturally went to the queen, and the whole swindle came apart.

Cardinal Rohan was arrested and thrown into the Bastille prison. The countess was brought back to France, publicly flogged, and was branded on each shoulder with a "V" (for *voleuse*, the French word for "thief"). She was then given a life's sentence in a women's prison. Her husband was never caught.

The commoners in France, who had had enough of the royal family's extravagant tastes and were about to rebel, demanded the release of the cardinal. They refused to believe the innocence of Marie Antoinette, and history books give us the rest of the story.

But, what happened to the pieces of the infamous necklace? It is said that the Duchess of Sutherland acquired twenty-two strands and that the Duke of Dorset had several of the diamonds. A flamboyant American, "Diamond Jim" Brady, bought one of the large tassels for actress Lillian Russell. Nothing was ever heard of the other pieces.

Cardinal Rohan's family, who considered it their duty to pay for the necklace, spent one hundred years paying back every cent to the jewelers and their heirs.

7.

DIAMONDS IN THE NEW WORLD

A s you might expect, diamonds were slow to find their place in the New World. The settlers who came to America were not the aristocratic and wealthy Europeans, and they brought no jewels with them. Worse yet, the Puritans in the Massachusetts Colony and the Quakers in Philadelphia were so opposed to self-adornment of any kind that they forbade the wearing of even a plain gold wedding band.

The Dutch settlers in New York were less severe. Jewelry stores, with gems imported from Europe, were already springing up there before 1700. Dutch girls wore glittering earrings below their little Dutch caps, and a few had rings of gold set with tiny jewels such as diamonds. The first diamond of any size, an unset solitaire, arrived in New York in 1764, but it wasn't recorded whether it was used to decorate a lady's hand or a man's buckle. There is almost no record of diamond rings in early America. It is known, however, that George Washington gave his wife a watch with diamond hands.

First Lady Dolley Madison was the first woman in

America known to have been obsessed with owning jewels. Even during the British blockade during the War of 1812, her fashionable clothes and jewels arrived successfully from Paris. Although she was reared a Quaker, she was excommunicated by her church when she married James Madison, who was not a Quaker. She put aside her plain gray bonnet and instead wore turbans decorated with feathers and jewels. At the fancy balls she loved, she always wore one decorated with a crescent of brilliant diamonds.

The First Ladies who followed Dolley were not fashion leaders nor party givers. In the 1840s, however, President Tyler's wife re-established the lavish White House balls. First Lady Julia Tyler presided over these affairs seated on a raised platform, like a queen on a throne. She wore a dazzling diamond tiara on her head, and she was surrounded by twelve "ladies-in-waiting."

Wealthy ladies all over began demanding diamonds, and Tiffany and Young, a New York jewelry store, began importing great quantities of them. Interest in such luxuries came to a temporary halt when the Civil War broke out in 1861.

By the 1890s, ladies were wearing diamond jewelry of all kinds. Even a few men sported the gems in their cuff links or scarf pins. John Warne Gates, who had made a fortune in the steel industry, wore diamonds on his shirtfront and on each suspender buckle, even in the daytime.

The most famous diamond lover during this time, however, was "Diamond Jim" Brady. He made millions selling

The actress Lillian Russell was known as "The American Beauty" in the era called the Gay Nineties. She was a close companion of Diamond Jim Brady, and was noted for her flamboyant personality and love of jewelry.

railway equipment and spent much of his fortune on diamonds and other jewels. It was said that he owned more than twenty thousand diamonds and would wear as many as $250,000 worth on a single day.

Brady had jewelry sets of studs, cuff links, belt buckles, scarf pins, and watch fobs for special occasions, such as when he went to the race track. For really grand affairs, he had a set made only of jewels once worn by Napoleon. In the most unusual one, his railroad set, each diamond-studded piece was a railroad car such as a coal car, a tank car, etc.

Just as Elizabeth I of England and Francis I of France did, Brady loved to scratch windowpanes with a diamond ring. He had no difficulty getting appointments with potential customers, because everyone was eager to see his diamonds. At the end of an appointment, he would go to the nearest window and scratch his name, James Buchanan Brady, on the glass with his ring. His signature on a window was a much-prized memento.

Many of Brady's diamonds were not for his personal adornment but for the love of his life, Lillian Russell, a famous actress of that time. He not only supplied her with jewelry to wear, but also gave her a diamond-studded bicycle. It was said that he gave her garters studded with diamonds.

Brady wasn't attempting to influence men's fashions, but in a way, he did. His display of huge diamonds in jewelry that wasn't even very attractive was considered vulgar. Many men became afraid to be seen wearing diamonds. Even the ladies were told that it was in poor taste to wear their gems in the daytime.

Another eccentric who loved diamonds was a jeweler named Herb Bales of Fairfield, Ohio. He had two diamonds set into his top front teeth.

During the last two decades of the nineteenth century, different styles of jewelry became popular. For a while the dog collar was the favorite style of necklace. This consisted of between four to nineteen strands of pearls, fastened together with a huge diamond clasp. Later, the strands themselves were of diamonds. Some ladies preferred a chain or single strand of gems that reached to their waist, or in some cases, to their knees.

A necklace of 18-carat gold with round diamonds set in a fluted shell motif, designed by the great Roman jewelry designer, Paolo Bulgari. Courtesy of GIA and Tino Hammid.

Next, the pearl or diamond bib became the rage. A network of jewels, it was 5 to 6 inches wide and about 5 inches long. Wealthy men had them custom-made for their wives. After a sketch was made of what they wanted, the stones or pearls were laid out on a sheet of wax. This was tried on the lady's neck to see whether she approved or wanted changes made. Usually a paste imitation of a diamond bib was made at the same time, for the lady to wear when traveling.

Fashionable ladies soon turned to the tiara, some of which contained as many as a thousand diamonds. These could be broken up into several sections that could be worn as pins, bracelets, or pendants. Bracelets didn't become popular until women no longer had to wear long sleeves.

The Everts Company of Dallas, Texas, is responsible for the fascination with charms. Rich Texans loved the miniature gold oil wells the company began producing in 1897. These were followed by bejeweled beer carts and rattlesnakes with diamond eyes. Many Texans wore the charms on their watch fobs; some gave them to their wives to wear on their wrists on a chain.

There is no way of knowing what interesting pieces of jewelry may have been lost in 1912. It is said that when the *Titanic* sank, it had on board $180 million worth of gold, and diamonds worth about $277 million.

The diamond engagement ring, with its large solitaire, was also gaining in popularity at around the turn of the century. No one can say for sure when this custom of giving rings began, but in the time of Julius Caesar (100 B.C.- 44 B.C.), young women were given an iron ring to seal a proposal of marriage.

The next authenticated use of an engagement ring is not until 1477, when Maximilian I, archduke of Austria, gave a diamond ring as a betrothal gift to Princess Mary of Burgundy. From then on, there is almost no mention of such a ring again until it became popular in nineteeth century America. The twentieth-century advertising campaign of the De Beers Corporation with its slogan, "A Diamond Is Forever," made the purchase of a diamond engagement ring in this country almost a necessity. The rest of the world has been slower to succumb to the advertising, however. It is only in Europe and Japan that the popularity of the diamond engagement ring is gaining strength rapidly.

A recent survey determined that more than three out of every four brides in our country receive a diamond engagement ring, but most hold a stone of less than half a carat. A one-carat stone is usually worth about three times as much as a half-carat one. Prices for stones of the same size differ greatly, however, because everything depends upon what are known as the four Cs: the cut, the weight in carats, the color, and the clarity.

During World War I, diamond purchases slowed to a trickle but afterward, largely due to the influence of the Hollywood stars, they took off again. Unfortunately, many of the stars, and the young ladies who mimicked them, had almost as bad taste as Diamond Jim. They wore diamonds with their slacks, their bathing suits, and their negligees. They wore diamonds on their ankles and even, at times, on their toes.

Since World War II, we have rarely seen the rich wearing very expensive jewelry pieces. If they have them, they are usually kept in vaults, and the ladies wear paste imitations.

Movie stars, particularly glamorous ones, have popularized diamond jewelry. Here the great Italian actress Sophia Loren wears a double diamond "riviere" necklace and diamond cluster earrings with pear-shaped drops.

Gwyneth Paltrow, holding her Oscar for Best Actress in Shakespeare in Love, *wears a 40-carat diamond princess necklace, custom-designed, and 6-carat diamond signature cluster earrings.* Both courtesy of the Diamond Information Center on behalf of De Beers.

Elizabeth Taylor has an extensive jewel collection, and it isn't always certain whether she is wearing the real thing or not. The actor Richard Burton, one of her many husbands, gave her a 33.19-carat diamond in 1969. Then, in 1972, he spent over $1 million on a pear-shaped 69.42-carat stone for her. At the same time, he had an imitation made of YAG, a diamond simulant. When the the Burtons' marriage broke up, Elizabeth sold the diamond to a Texas oil millionaire for $2.8 million. He sold it again shortly afterward and commented that he had made a nice profit.

There have been even more expensive diamonds on the market in this century. The day after the stock market crash of October 1988, a 64.83-carat diamond pendant sold for $6,380,000. Generally, diamonds that sell in the million bracket are not for wearing, but for investment. Many people like to purchase even less expensive diamonds as a hedge against inflation.

Diamonds are a very important commodity for people in troubled areas of the world who have to flee their homes without taking many belongings. Gold has been used too, but it is heavy and hard to carry. A fortune in diamonds can be carried in just a small pocket. People escaping from Germany before World War II used this means to be sure of having something to get them started in their new home. Many refugees who came to the United States from places such as Cuba and Vietnam did likewise.

Although you wouldn't expect to hear any amusing stories concerning diamonds, there was a rather funny incident that took place in our country during the Great Depression. Harpo Marx, the comedian, went into a fancy jewelry store in New York and asked to see some loose diamonds. As he was well-known, he probably wasn't watched as carefully by the guards as someone else would have been. Suddenly, he made a dash for the door. Two guards were close on his heels, and when he was tackled by them, loose stones fell out of his pockets and scattered all over the street. The stones, which Harpo had picked up elsewhere, were absolutely worthless. He had pulled the stunt to win a bet he had made with a friend.

8.

ADVENTURE, INTRIGUE, AND MURDER

Some of today's diamonds are famous because of the amount of money paid for them. More interesting than sheer monetary value, however, are the histories of some of the old stones—tales of adventure, intrigue, and even murder.

The first European to see some of the famous old Indian stones was the French traveler and gem merchant, Jean Baptiste Tavernier. Between 1631 and 1668 he made six trips to India, Persia, and Turkey. Sometimes spending as long as five years on a single trip, he visited the ruling monarchs of each land and was allowed to look at their huge collections of great jewels. He bought those that he could, and he made sketches and wrote detailed descriptions of the most spectacular of the others. This was indeed fortunate, because many of the great gems have never been seen since. Some are known to have been recut; a few may be resting in some hidden treasure house in the East, or even in Europe.

THE KOH-I-NOOR, MOUNTAIN OF LIGHT

The most famous of the Indian diamonds described by Tavernier, and the one with the longest and bloodiest history,

Jean Baptiste Tavernier

was the Koh-i-noor. It is believed to have been in royal crowns of India as long as 5,000 years ago, but its authenticated history begins in 1304. At that time it reportedly weighed almost 800 carats (about five and one-half ounces) and belonged to the Rajah of Malwa. It had been in his family for several hundred years and already had the bad reputation of bringing disaster to anyone who owned it.

In 1304 the Rajah of Malwa was conquered by a Turkish sultan and had to give up his favorite gem. The sultan was murdered in 1316, and his descendants had the huge rough stone cut and reduced to a mere 186 carats.

In 1526 Baber, founder of the Mogul Empire, conquered India and acquired the famous diamond. For two centuries it was inherited by each succeeding Mogul emperor including Shah Jahan, who built the famous Taj Mahal Palace in India around the middle of the seventeenth century. His greedy son Aurangzeb seized the throne, threw his father in prison, and had his three brothers killed to keep them from getting the Koh-i-noor.

When the Persians defeated the Moguls in 1739, their ruler, Nadir Shah, searched in vain for the fabulous diamond. Then he learned that the last Mogul emperor, Mohammed Shah, had concealed it in the turban that he always wore.

Nadir invited the Mogul to dinner and suggested that they exchange turbans. As it was a tradition for rulers of equal rank to do this on state occasions, Mohammed dared not refuse. When Nadir was finally alone, he began unwinding the yards and yards of silk. When the diamond fell to the floor he

Shah Jahan

gasped and exclaimed, "Koh-i-noor" ("Mountain of Light" in his language), and that was the stone's name from then on.

Nadir Shah was assassinated by a member of his bodyguard in 1747. When his successor, Shah Rukh, refused to reveal the whereabouts of the famous diamond, his eyes were put out and boiling oil poured over his head by a rebellious Arab chieftain. He was finally deposed and imprisoned. His successor Ahmed Shah, founder of the Afghan dynasty, killed the Arab chieftain and offered Shah Rukh his freedom in exchange for the Koh-i-noor. The shah surrendered the gem.

Ahmed Shah left the diamond to his son, who bequeathed it to his son, Zaman Shah, in 1793. It brought bad luck again when Zaman was blinded, deposed, and imprisioned by his brother, Shah Shuja, but he managed to hide the gem in the mud walls of his prison cell. Shortly, however, it was found and given to the new shah. He wore the Koh-i-noor pinned to his breast at all ceremonies.

Shah Shuja was later blinded and dethroned by his nephew, Shah Mahmud, but somehow managed to retain the great diamond. In 1833, he took it and Zaman, the brother he had blinded, and fled to the court of Runjit-Singh in Punjab, a region of India. Shah Shuja had to surrender the Koh-i-noor to his protector, who had it set in a bracelet he wore on special occasions. When Runjit died in 1839, the bracelet was placed in the national treasury at Lahore, the capital of Punjab.

Ten years of civil unrest followed, during which time at least one of Runjit's successors was murdered.

In 1849, when the British annexed Punjab to their other conquests in India, the Koh-i-noor came into the possession of the East India Company. A year later it was presented as a gift to Queen Victoria. Because it had been so poorly cut, she had it recut and reduced to 108.93 carats. As it was not supposed to bring bad luck to women, Victoria wore it; then Queen Mary; and it was finally set in the crown of Queen Elizabeth (the mother of Queen Elizabeth II). This crown is now on display with the British royal jewels in the Tower of London.

THE GREAT CROWN JEWEL ROBBERY

When Louis XV was crowned King of France in 1722, he wore the most spectacular crown ever seen. Covered with pearls, diamonds, and other precious stones, it featured two huge gems—the Regent, a diamond of 140 carats, and the Sancy, one of 55 carats. After the coronation these two were removed for safekeeping and glass copies put in their place on the crown.

During the French Revolution (1792-1802), thieves broke into the locked cabinet where the crown jewels and other royal treasures were stored. The Regent was found fifteen months later in the attic of a house in Paris, but neither the Sancy nor the French Blue, another famous diamond, were ever found. It is believed that the latter was recut into three stones, one of which is the famous Hope diamond.

THE REGENT

Even before it joined the crown jewels of France, the Regent had an interesting history. The story begins in 1701 in the diamond mines of India. A slave came across a huge diamond of 410 carats and decided to try to keep it for himself. Knowing that he would be searched as he left the mine, he slashed his leg with a sharp knife and hid the diamond in the cloth he tied around it. The searchers didn't discover it, and he was allowed to leave.

The slave found his way to the coast and offered the skipper of a British boat half the value of the stone in exchange for his ocean passage. Not far out of port, the captain took possession of the diamond and had the slave thrown overboard. The captain sold the stone to an Indian merchant, gambled away his money, and ended up by hanging himself.

The diamond was bought by Thomas Pitt, the English

governor of Madras in India, and for many years it was known as the Pitt diamond. When Pitt returned to England, he tried to sell the gem to several European sovereigns, but all thought his asking price was too high.

Pitt changed from a happy-go-lucky fellow into a recluse who tried to avoid even his friends. He was afraid to let anyone see the diamond. He put it under his pillow each night and kept a loaded pistol nearby. He seldom slept two consecutive nights under the same roof and usually wore a disguise whenever he went out.

Finally in 1717 the diamond was purchased for Louis XV by the duke of Orleans, regent of France until the young Louis was old enough to take over the reign. That was when it became known as the Regent diamond.

When Napoleon was crowned Emperor of France in 1804, he had the diamond set in the hilt of his ceremonial sword. When he was forced into exile on the island of Elba, the Regent began traveling again. Eventually it returned to France and was placed in the Louvre Museum in Paris, where it has been on display ever since.

THE SANCY

The early history of the Regent's companion in the royal crown is pretty much a mystery. It must have come from India but no one knows when, or what the rough stone weighed. The Seigneur de Sancy, French ambassador to Turkey, bought it in Constantinople in about 1570. Back in

France, he lent it to King Henry III to wear on the cap he used to cover his baldness.

After the king was assassinated, his successor, Henry IV, asked to borrow the diamond. The messenger who was carrying the stone to court disappeared, and news reached the king that he had been waylaid and murdered. Sancy, who had complete trust in his servant, felt sure the man would never have allowed thieves to get their hands on the diamond. He went to the forest where the slaying had taken place, found the servant's body, and had an autopsy performed. The diamond was found in his stomach, safe from the eyes of the highwaymen.

Rather than lend the diamond again, Sancy sold it to Queen Elizabeth I of England. It stayed there until the overthrow of James II in 1690, when it returned to France and was stolen with the other crown jewels.

THE ORLOFF

The most often told story about this famous gem begins in the early eighteenth century on a river island in southern India. In the innermost shrine of a Hindu temple stood the statue of a god whose eyes were huge diamonds.

A French soldier, a deserter who lived in the area, won the friendship of the Hindu priests by showing deep interest in their religion. He was given the job of guardian of the inner temple. One night he pried out one of the diamond eyes, swam across the river with it, and escaped through

THE WORLD'S LARGEST ROUGH DIAMONDS

	Carats	Name	When found	Where found
1.	3,106.0	Cullinan	1905	South Africa
2.	995.2	Excelsior	1893	South Africa
3.	968.9	Star of Sierra Leone	1972	Sierra Leone
4.	890.0	Golden Triolette, or The Incomparable Diamond	?	West Africa?
5.	793.0	Great Mogul	1650	India
6.	770.0	Woyie River	1945	Sierra Leone
7.	726.6	Vargas	1938	Brazil
8.	726.0	Jonker	1934	South Africa
9.	650.3	Reitz	1895	South Africa
10.	616.0	Kimberly Octahedron	1974	South Africa
11.	609.3	Baumgold	1923	South Africa
12.	601.3	Lesotho	1967	Lesotho
13.	600.0	Goyaz	1906	Brazil
14.	572.3	Unnamed	1955	South Africa
15.	532.0	Unnamed	1943	Sierra Leone
16.	527.0	Unnamed	1965	Lesotho
17.	516.5	Kimberley Rough	1896	South Africa
18.	511.3	Venter	1951	South Africa
19.	509.6	Unnamed	1976	Sierra Leone
20.	469.0	Victoria	1884	South Africa

Figure 3

the jungle to Madras. There he sold it to an English sea captain.

The diamond turned up later in Amsterdam and was bought by a Russian prince, Gregory Orloff. He was once the favorite of Empress Catherine the Great, but she had lost interest in him. In an attempt to win back her affections, he gave the empress the nearly 200-carat gem. She accepted it happily but would have nothing more to do with the prince. The diamond was mounted in the royal scepter where it still exists today among the treasures in the Kremlin.

THE CULLINAN

On the whole, diamonds found in Africa have been larger than Indian diamonds. Some of the famous large African stones are the 995-carat Excelsior (found unexpectedly in a shovelful of dirt), the 968-carat Star of Sierra Leone, the 726-carat Jonker, and the 650-carat Jubilee. The 467-carat Victoria is famous not only for size, but because it appeared in a movie, *Tarzan's Savage Fury*, as the eye of a jungle god.

By far the largest diamond found in Africa, or anywhere in the world, came to light in 1905 in an open pit mine in Transvaal, at that time a country bordering on South Africa. The mine superintendent was making his daily inspection when something in one of the side walls flashed in the setting sun. He thought it was a piece of glass put there by a practical joker. However, he took his pocket knife and pried the thing out. It was a stone almost the size of his fist: 4 inches long, 2¼ inches

Models of the Cullinan diamond in the rough, and the nine major stones that were cut from it. Courtesy of De Beers.

wide, and 2½ inches high. He sent it to be analyzed and learned that it was a diamond weighing 3,106 carats (about a pound and a half)—blue white and nearly flawless.

The huge stone was named the Cullinan for the president of the mining company, Sir Thomas Cullinan. After purchasing the diamond, the Transvaal government presented it to England's King Edward VII on his sixty-sixth birthday. It was mailed to the mining company's London office by ordinary parcel post while a fake diamond was taken aboard a steamer with great fanfare and heavily guarded during the voyage.

King Edward felt that the massive chunk should be di-

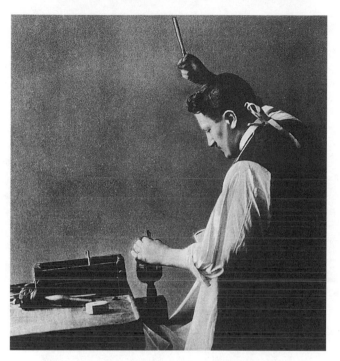

Josef Asscher cleaving the Cullinan diamond on February 10, 1908, in Amsterdam. Courtesy of De Beers.

vided into several smaller gems and hired the famous Dutch cutter from Amsterdam, Joseph Asscher, to do the job. After studying the stone for several months, he made a groove on one edge, placed his wedge there and, perspiring freely, struck it with his mallet. The steel blade broke instead of the diamond.

Asscher fainted as he hit the stone a second time. When he came to, he found that the great diamond had split precisely as he had planned. After further cleaving, the cutter had nine major gems and ninety-six smaller ones.

Head of Sceptre with Cross. Made in 1661 for the coronation of Charles II, since 1910 it has contained the First Star of Africa, cut from the Cullinan diamond and believed to be the largest cut diamond in the world until recently. Courtesy of The HMSO Collection, the Crown Jewels.

The principal stone weighed 530.2 carats and was the largest cut diamond in the world until 1988, when a diamond cutter produced a golden-colored gem of 531 carats. The largest of the Cullinan stones was named the Great Star of Africa and was set in the English royal scepter. The second largest cut, the Lesser Star of Africa, weighed

The Imperial State Crown of England, made in 1937 for the coronation of George VI as a replica of the crown made for Queen Victoria in 1838. It contains the St. Edward's Sapphire in the Maltese Cross at the top; the Black Prince's Ruby at the front, and, underneath this, the Second Star of Africa, which was cut from the Cullinan diamond. Courtesy of The HMSO Collection, the Crown Jewels.

317.4 carats and is mounted in the Imperial State Crown of England.

During World War II, when German aircraft were bombing the city of London, the gems were removed from their settings and hidden in a lake with the other crown jewels at Windsor Castle. Only King George VI (Queen Elizabeth II's father) and one of his trusted employees knew of the hiding place. After the war, the jewels were returned to the Tower of London for everyone to admire.

THE HOPE

Probably the best known gem in the world is the Hope diamond, which is on display in the Smithsonian Institution in Washington, D.C.

When it first became famous, it belonged to King Louis XIV of France and was called the Blue Diamond of the Crown. It has also been referred to as the French Blue or Tavernier's Blue (for the merchant who sold it to King Louis XIV).

There was a rumor that Tavernier had stolen it from a statue of Rama Sita and that the god had put a curse on anyone who owned it in the future. Tavernier did no such thing, although he might have bought it from someone who did steal it. Anyway, the story of this diamond's evil spell persisted for four centuries.

The diamond, of a rare deep blue color, weighed 112 carats when Tavernier brought it from India in 1668, but Louis had it recut to 67.5 carats. The gem was blamed for every misfortune that befell its royal owners—even Louis XV's fatal case of smallpox and the beheading of his successor.

The Blue was stolen with the other crown jewels in 1792

and, unlike the Regent, was never found. In 1830 a 44.5-carat blue diamond turned up in London without any of the usual information about its origin or previous owners. Because of its very rare color, its size and its shape, gemologists feel certain that it was cut from the French Blue.

A London banker, Henry Philip Hope, bought the diamond, and it passed down to a descendant named Francis Pelham Clinton Hope. This was when the series of misfortunes blamed on the Hope diamond began. Hope got into serious financial difficulties because of his gambling and had to sell the diamond. His wife, an American actress named May Yohe, ran off with another man. Hope accidentally shot himself in the leg while hunting and had to have the limb amputated. His second wife died a few years after their wedding. Even May Yohe, who was left with only a replica of the famous gem to wear for her stage performances, supposedly suffered all sorts of misfortunes.

There are several stories about the diamond's travels after Hope sold it in 1901 and before it came to America in 1910. The first dealer who bought it went mad and committed suicide. A Russian prince, to whom it belonged, loaned it to a dancer and she was shot onstage by a jealous rival. A Greek jeweler who looked at the stone drove off a cliff, killing himself and his family. After the Sultan of Turkey bought the diamond, he was deposed. So go the stories, but many of them are either untrue or greatly exaggerated.

The authenticated history begins again when an American woman, Evalyn Walsh McLean, bought the blue stone in

Paris in 1910. She was told the stories about it, but said she felt that bad luck objects were lucky for her. She had it mounted on a chain of sixty-two matched diamonds and wore it everywhere.

Though Mrs. McLean had more than her share of troubles, she never blamed the diamond. In addition to the tragic and early death of her brother, her nine-year-old son was hit and killed by a car, and her daughter died from an overdose of sleeping pills. Her husband went insane and died in a mental institution.

After her death, the New York jeweler Harry Winston bought the diamond from her estate. He exhibited it around the country and raised millions of dollars for charitable causes. Finally, in 1958 he presented the Hope to the Smithsonian.

Most people feel that the beautiful diamond had nothing to do with anyone's misfortunes, but there are those who want to believe in the curse and feel that it is a permanent part of the stone. They like to point out such things as an incident that happened in 1975. Actor Rod Serling, who narrated "The Legendary Curse of the Hope Diamond" for a television special, died a few months later during surgery. Was this just a coincidence?

9.

DIAMONDS AT WORK

Only 20 percent of the diamonds mined today go into jewelry. The other 80 percent—those that are badly flawed, poorly shaped, discolored, or too small—are used in industry. So many industrial diamonds are needed, however, that only 20 percent of the total used are natural stones; the rest are synthetic.

It is known that diamonds were already working for people in early times. The Chinese used diamonds to cut and carve lovely jade objects. The stones were important in early metalworking trades. They were used especially in engraving, for drilling holes in things like pearls, and for doing fine work of all kinds.

It seems unlikely that the beautiful stone carving of Indian and Moorish architecture could have been produced without this very hard cutting tool. In many of the buildings, the stone is cut into such intricate and tiny openings that the walls look like lace.

Diamonds are so widely used today that most of our important industries would come to a standstill if the supply suddenly ran out.

The giant saw blade used in this heavy construction work is edged with diamonds.
Courtesy of CIMLINE Company.

CUTTING AND SAWING

Diamond-edged wheels or saws are used for cutting glass, gems, stone of all kinds, and metals. They cut faster, produce less heat from friction, and last longer than tools from early times. They are essential to aircraft and automotive industries where they shape pistons and other parts of engines rapidly and accurately. They cut patterns of all kinds in machine shops.

In heavy construction work, large saws up to 8 feet in

diameter cut stone blocks for bridges and carve huge slabs for monuments. In contrast, there are diamond saws small enough to cut grooves in the tiniest of screws. Before laser surgery was developed, diamond-edged scalpels produced the fine incisions necessary in eye surgery.

For many cutting tools, the diamonds have to be shaped by an expert in much the same way as a gemstone. It is important to get the best cutting edge possible on each stone. Naturally they must also be set in the tool in the best possible position.

GRINDING AND POLISHING

The diamond has become the most important industrial abrasive of the twentieth century. Inferior natural stones (called "bort") or synthetic diamonds are crushed to form various grades of grit or powder. Different sizes are needed for different jobs.

Grinding wheels are the main use for crushed bort. Here, too, the bonding of the stones to the tool is important in order to insure that the maximum number of sharp edges are exposed. The wheels are used to grind and polish gems, glass, ceramics, and metals.

Diamond powder, which can be finer than household flour, is mixed with oil, powdered metal, or ceramic material to form a paste. This polishes lenses, many precision instruments, and even dental fillings, without leaving any scratches.

DRILLING

Of all the ways in which diamonds are used in industry, they have probably had the most revolutionary effects in heavy drilling. When pneumatic drills (jackhammers) were used on roads or buildings under construction, the noise was deafening. With diamond-set bits, drilling can be done in the middle of the night without awakening anyone in nearby houses.

For a long time it was necessary to shape holes and tunnels for plumbing or wires in new buildings while the concrete was still wet. Diamond drills now do the work quickly after the concrete has become hard. They also bore holes in solid rock to dig wells or make tunnels.

The oil industry has great need for diamond bits, which have increased oil production almost tenfold. They not only do the work faster but last much longer than the old drills. A diamond bit is good for about 200 hours whereas the metal bit wears out after some thirty hours. This is especially important because it can take as long as eighteen hours to change the bit on a rock drill in a well.

Diamond bits have also been found useful in taking core samples of rock below roads and bridges to see if they are still safe. To prevent cracks in a dam from getting worse, small holes are made and a filler forced into these to seal the dam. A diamond-tipped drill is used because it causes almost no vibration.

/PECIAL U/E/

Diamond-coated tools have contributed to our safety in other ways too. They have been used to cut grooves in roads and airport runways to make them skidproof. The same tools can be used to smooth down dangerous bumps.

One of the most important uses of industrial diamonds is as dies used for making the fine wire needed in a wrist watch, radio, or TV set, and for the filaments in a light bulb. Laser beams drill tiny holes of different sizes in the stones, and the wire is pulled through these. Progressively smaller holes are used until the wire is of the desired thickness. It takes a lot longer for the holes in these diamond dies to widen from use than it used to take in metal dies.

The space industry has been very dependent on diamonds for their ability to shape accurately the different parts of the spacecraft. The *Pioneer* spacecraft launched toward Venus in 1978 even had a transparent diamond as a porthole. It was especially chosen from among thousands of excellent stones and was cut in such a way as to give it maximum strength combined with maximum visibility. Scientists decided that diamond was the only material that could survive a four-month journey through space and the climate of Venus, which has searing heat, crushing pressure (100 times that of Earth's atmosphere), and an extremely corrosive atmosphere containing carbon dioxide and sulphuric acid.

Diamonds are excellent thermal conductors, and they have been very useful in industry in spotting temperature changes in electrical instruments. A diamond thermometer can instantly detect changes as small as one-thousandth of a degree.

ALWAYS SOMETHING NEW

Scientists are forever trying to find new uses for diamonds as well as to improve upon the quality of the stones themselves. In 1990 researchers discovered how to improve, by 50 percent, the ability of synthetic diamonds to conduct heat.

They can withstand ten times more laser energy than ordinary diamonds. This opened up new possibilities for two of our country's most important technologies—electronics and communications.

The major problem to be overcome when diamonds were first used in industry was how to fasten the stones or powder to tools. Clamping or brazing (similar to soldering) answered some of the problems, but not all.

It is now possible to "grow" thin films of diamond on different substances. One of several processes involves heating the base material to a very high temperature in a furnace with carbon-containing gases. The heat decomposes the carbon molecules, and they are deposited on the base material as diamonds.

These new diamond films are important in the production of transistors and computer chips, which at first relied upon silicon as the basic raw material. As diamond conducts heat far better than silicon, it means that the components in a computer can be more tightly packed. This leads to the ability to make smaller yet more powerful computers.

We will probably see many objects coated with diamond

films around our house some day, too—kitchen utensils that never need sharpening, razor blades that last forever, coated windows that will be impossible to scratch. Right now the closest you will come to an industrial diamond is when your dentist drills a hole to fill a cavity in your tooth!

10.

GOOD LUCK OR BAD?

From very early times, people have regarded precious stones with awe and reverence. They have attributed to them powers unlike those of anything else in nature.

Stories of their magical abilities abound in the sacred writings of the Hebrews, the ancient Egyptians, the Babylonians, the Arabs, and the Chinese.

During the Middle Ages and even down to the seventeenth century, the belief in the special virtues of precious stones was held by both members of the upper classes and by peasants, by the learned as well as the uneducated, by the pious and by the nonreligious.

Although many people believe that precious stones first became popular because of their beauty and were used only as objects of adornment, scholars feel that the stones were first used purely as amulets or talismans (good luck charms). Whichever came first, people soon decided that it didn't detract from the magical power of the stones to be set in beautiful necklaces, bracelets, or rings, and that was the best way to keep the charms with them.

THE GREAT PROTECTOR

Every gemstone has been used as an amulet, but few have had as many powers attributed to them as has the diamond. In the Middle Ages, it was believed that wearing a diamond would protect one against ghosts and prevent nightmares, especially when it was set in gold and worn on the left arm. A diamond could also counteract the evil eye and all spells by enchanters.

Most important of all, the diamond was the emblem of fearlessness and strength, bringing victory in battle. At a famous trial in 1232, Hubert de Burgh, a court official of King Henry III of England, was charged with having stolen from his sovereign a valuable stone which rendered the wearer invincible in battle. Worse yet, he had given it to Henry's enemy, the king of Wales. There doesn't seem to be any explanation of what would have happened if two men in single combat had each worn a diamond for protection.

In some cultures it was believed that diamonds could even predict an outcome in battle. The Old Testament mentions that the high priest of Israel wore a breastplate set with twelve precious stones. According to the Jewish historian Josephus, who believed they were diamonds, their radiance always intensified just before the armies of Israel won a battle.

In ancient India where diamonds were plentiful, it was said that anyone who gave a diamond to a religious shrine would be assured of eternal life.

MEDICINAL USES

In every period of history, precious and semiprecious stones have been used both as amulets to prevent illness and as cures for certain ailments from simple bellyache to a serious wound. Topaz, for example, had the reputation of curing eye diseases. It was marinated in wine for three days and then rubbed across a patient's eyes.

As a good health charm, the diamond was said to give protection against the plague and many minor ailments. It protected the wearer from poisons. Particles given off from the poisonous material supposedly gathered on the surface of the stone and could be wiped off. To get the maximum benefit from diamonds, people always wore them on the left side of the body, or so-called "heart side."

Drinking water in which a diamond had been dipped was another good way of preventing illnesses, especially gout, jaundice, and apoplexy. Wearing a diamond set in a gold bracelet was a popular remedy for leprosy or insanity.

Sometimes precious stones were taken internally. Ground-up emeralds were given as a laxative in India, and diamond powder from unflawed stones was supposed to guarantee strength, energy, beauty, clear skin, happiness, and longevity. In Europe, in the Middle Ages, physicians regularly prescribed crushed diamonds as an antidote for poison. Charles VI of France was given a mixture of diamonds and other gemstones to swallow as he lay dying, but they didn't save his life.

During the sixteenth century, when diamonds were common among royalty, the members of the upper class began giving up their superstitious beliefs about gems. Not the other levels of society, however. People of the lower classes frequently borrowed jewelry set with diamonds in order to press the stones against an afflicted part of the body. It was easy for those who could not possess this rare stone to credit it with supernatural abilities.

DEADLY POISON?

Strangely, the very stone that was used for the prevention against and cure for poisoning also came to be considered by many a deadly poison itself. Perhaps this was due to a renewed interest in ancient legends. In several cultures it was told that the diamond had been "born" in a faraway land guarded by venomous creatures. As they crawled around, they were scratched by the sharp stones, and some of their poison trickled onto the diamonds.

The Turkish sultan Bejazet II (1447–1512) is said to have been murdered by his son Selim, who put pulverized diamonds into his father's food. There is also the story of the famous Italian goldsmith Benvenuto Cellini. One day while he was imprisoned in Rome in 1538, he felt some hard particles in the food he was eating. Then he noticed some shiny bits on his plate. He panicked at the thought that he had swallowed ground diamonds and was sure that he would die. He didn't, to his surprise.

After his release from prison, Cellini learned that an enemy had hired a gem cutter to grind a diamond into dust so it could be put into his food. The gem cutter was very poor, so he sold the diamond and ground up another kind of stone in its place. Cellini was sure that he had barely escaped being killed, and he probably had. Ground diamonds would have the same effect on the stomach as ground glass.

Mine owners were very happy to have their superstitious workers believe in the diamond's poisonous qualities. It kept them from swallowing valuable stones which they could recover later.

NOT JUST ANY OLD DIAMOND

Though diamonds were thought to have tremendous powers as amulets, not just any old stone would do. A stone that wasn't perfect, one that was off-color or flawed in any way, could cause great misfortune to its owner.

The original shape was important during the early days before diamonds were cut and polished. A stone shaped like a pyramid was said to cause quarrels. A square-shaped diamond could cause mental anguish. The worst of all, a five-cornered stone might even cause death.

The Hindus especially were afraid of an imperfect diamond and believed it could cause such ailments as lameness, jaundice, pleurisy, and leprosy. They even felt that such a stone might keep them from reaching their highest heaven.

During the Middle Ages people believed that even a

perfect diamond could lose its protective power if it were handled, or even gazed upon, by an impure person. Certain gems set in holy statues were said to have jumped out of their settings when a sin was committed in their presence. Any diamond acquired by theft would be sure to bring misfortune upon its owner. Religious rites were often used to counteract any evil spell that had been put on a diamond and restore its original magical properties.

Through the ages people have believed that to be really effective as an amulet, a diamond should never be acquired by purchase. It must be given as a token of love or friendship if its new owner is to have the use of its magical virtues. How wonderful it would be if every diamond bought for a loved one today would bring happiness ever after!

GLOJJARY

Alluvial—riverbed

Blue ground—kimberlite

Blue-white—term used to describe a diamond that is almost completely devoid of color

Bort—inferior diamonds which are crushed to form grit or powder

Bruting—polishing by rubbing two diamonds together

Carat—unit of weight equal to $\frac{1}{142}$ of an ounce

Carbonado—black, extremely hard diamond of great value in industry

Carob—bean used as unit of weight for diamonds before the metric carat

Cradle—rocking device used for washing gold or diamonds out of the soil

Cyclotron—circular accelerator used to generate subatomic particles

Diamonaire—a manmade stone of xttriam aluminum that closely resembles diamond

Dispersion—breaking up of light into spectrum colors

Dodecahedron—a crystal with twelve faces

Fabulite—a manmade stone of strontium titanate that closely resembles diamond

Facet—small flat surface produced by cutting a diamond or other precious stone

Fancy—a diamond that has a natural, pleasing color

Fire—flashes of separate colors

Fluorescent—glowing under ultraviolet light

Hardness—resistance to scratching or chipping

Igneous rock—rock formed by cooling and solidification of a molten magma

Inclusion—a small crystal of some mineral that grew inside the diamond

Kimberlite—igneous rock in which diamonds are found

Lamproite—igneous rock very simiar to kimberlte

Lapidaries—workers who cut and polish gemstones

Long Tom—trough used for washing gold or diamonds out of the soil

Luster—the quality of light reflected from the diamond's surface

Nuclear reactor—device used to bring about a reaction in which the nucleus of an element changes

Octahedron—a crystal with eight faces, that looks like two square-based pyramids put together

Olivine crystal—a semiprecious stone

Opaque—allowing no light to pass through the stone

Paste—a hard, brilliant glass containing lead oxide that closely resembles diamond

Phosphorescent—continuing to glow for a long time after being exposed to ultraviolet light

Refraction—the bending of light rays

Simulant—a mineral that, when colorless, looks almost like a diamond

Synthetic—manmade

Thermal conductivity—capability of conducting heat

Translucent—allowing light to pass through the stone

Windlass—rope used for hoisting, turned by a crank with a handle

YAG—a diamond simulant

Zircon—a mineral occurring in four-sided crystals that closely resembles diamond

RELATED READING

Titles marked with asterisks are for rockhounds. When looking for diamonds, you might want to know what other minerals can be found in the same area and how to identify them.

Bates, Robert L. *Industrial Minerals. How They Are Found and Used.* Hillside, New Jersey: Enslow Publishers, Inc. 1998. (64 pages. Black and white illustrations.)

*Duda, Rudolf and Lubos Rejl. *Minerals of the World.* New York: Arch Cape Press. 1984. (520 pages. Color illustrations.)

Heiniger, Ernst A. and Jean. *The Great Book of Jewels.* Boston: New York Graphic Society. 1974 (316 pages. Color illustrations. Famous pieces of jewelry through the ages, stories of famous diamonds and other gems, and more.)

Morris, Scott E., ed. *Using and Understanding Maps. Rocks and Minerals of the World.* New York: Chelsea House Publishers. 1993. (47 pages. Colored maps of the world showing the location of various minerals, fossils, volcanoes, and earthquakes with interesting facts about each.)

*Pough, Frederick. *Peterson Field Guide for Rocks and Minerals.* Boston: Houghton Mifflin. 1988. (396 pages. Color illustrations.)

*Sinkankas, John. *Field Collecting Gemstones and Minerals.* Tucson, Arizona: Geoscience Press. 1988. (397 pages. Black and white illustrations. One chapter on tools needed for rock collecting and how to use them.)

*Srogi, LeeAnn. *Rocks and Minerals.* Philadelphia: Running Press. 1989. (How to start collecting, equipment needed, and general information.)

ACKNOWLEDGMENTS

The author wishes to thank the following people, whose help made this book possible: Lewis S. Dean of the Geological Survey of Alabama; Alan J. Giles of the Georgia State Department of Natural Resources; Michael C. Hansen, Ph.D., of the Ohio State Department of Natural Resources; J. Michael Howard of the Arkansas State Geological Commission; John D. Marr, Jr., of the Virginia State Division of Mineral Resources; Dr. M.G. Mudrey, Jr., of the Wisconsin State Geological and Natural History Survey; Jenne A. Sewell of the North Carolina Department of Environmental and Natural Resources; Dale M. Stickney of the California State Division of Mines and Geology; Ronald P. Zurawski of the Tennessee State Department of Environment and Conservation, Division of Geology; Dona Dirlam, Elaine Ferrari-Santhon, Cathy Jonathan, and Ruth Patchick, research librarians at the Gemological Institute of America in Carlsbad, California; John Callahan and Jim Merzbacher, high school science teachers; and last but not least, my friends Barbara Rollins, Pamela Rundel, Ed Ehrhart, and Arvid Natwick, who helped with everything from computer problems to making sure I really knew what I was talking about.

INDEX

Pages with illustrations are in boldface.